Sports Media Relations

CAREERS
OFF THE FIELD

CAREERS OFF THE FIELD

Analytics: Sports Stats and More

Arena & Event Management

Coaching & Scouting

Health Careers in Sports

Sports Agent

Sports Broadcasting

Sports Marketing

Sports Media Relations

Sportswriting and Sports Photography

Working in College Sports

Sports
Media
Relations

By James Buckley Jr.

CAREERS
OFF THE FIELD

MC

Mason Crest

450 Parkway Drive, Suite D
Broomall, PA 19008
www.masoncrest.com

Printed and bound in the United States of America.

Series ISBN: 978-1-4222-3264-4
Hardback ISBN: 978-1-4222-3269-9
EBook ISBN: 978-1-4222-8527-5

First printing
1 3 5 7 9 8 6 4 2

Produced by Shoreline Publishing Group LLC
Santa Barbara, California

Editorial Director: James Buckley Jr.
Designer: Bill Madrid
Production: Sandy Gordon
www.shorelinepublishing.com
Cover photo: Dreamstime.com/Eric Broder Van Dyke

Library of Congress Cataloging-in-Publication Data is on file with the publisher

CONTENTS

Key Icons to Look For

Words to Understand: These words with their easy-to-understand definitions will increase the reader's understanding of the text, while building vocabulary skills.

Sidebars: This boxed material within the main text allows readers to build knowledge, gain insights, explore possibilities, and broaden their perspectives by weaving together additional information to provide realistic and holistic perspectives.

Research Projects: Readers are pointed toward areas of further inquiry connected to each chapter. Suggestions are provided for projects that encourage deeper research and analysis.

Text-Dependent Questions: These questions send the reader back to the text for more careful attention to the evidence presented here.

Series Glossary of Key Terms: This back-of-the-book glossary contains terminology used throughout this series. Words found here increase the reader's ability to read and comprehend higher-level books and articles in this field.

Foreword
By Al Ferrer

So you want to work in sports? Good luck! You've taken a great first step by picking up this volume of **CAREERS OFF THE FIELD.** I've been around sports professionally—on and off the field, in the front office, and in the classroom—for more than 35 years. My students have gone on to work in all the major sports leagues and for university athletic programs. They've become agents, writers, coaches, and broadcasters. They were just where you are now, and the lessons they learned can help you succeed.

One of the most important things to remember when looking for a job in sports is that being a sports fan is not enough. If you get an interview with a team, and your first sentence is "I'm your biggest fan," that's a kiss of death. They don't want fans, they want pros. Show your experience, show what you know, show how you can contribute.

Another big no-no is to say, "I'll do anything." That makes you a non-professional or a wanna-be. You have to do the research and find out what area is best for your personality and your skills. This book series will be a vital tool for you to do that research, to find out what areas in sports are out there, what kind of people work in them, and where you would best fit in.

And that leads to my third point: Know yourself. Look carefully at your interests and skills. You need to understand what you're good at and how you like to work. If you get energy from being around people, then you don't want to be in a room with a computer because you'll go nuts. You want to be in the action around people, so you might look at sales or marketing or media relations or being an agent. But if you're more comfortable being by yourself, then you look at analysis, research, perhaps the numbers side of scouting or recruiting. So you have to know yourself.

And you have to manage your expectations. There is a lot of money in sports but unless you are a star athlete, you probably won't be making much in your early years.

I'm not trying to be negative, but I want to be realistic. I've loved every minute of my life in sports. If you have a passion for sports and you can bring professionalism and quality work—and you understand your expectations—you can have a great career. But just like the athletes we admire, you have to prepare, you have to work hard, and you have to never, ever quit.

Series consultant Al Ferrer founded the sports management program at the University of California, Santa Barbara, after an award-winning career as a Division I baseball coach. Along with his work as a professor, Ferrer is an advisor to pro and college teams, athletes, and sports businesses.

Introduction

It's game night for the men's basketball team at the University of California, Santa Barbara (UCSB). Tip-off is hours away, but sports information director (SID) Bill Mahoney (left) has been at work since eight a.m. He won't be home until midnight. And in between, he's got a lot to do.

Like all sports media relations professionals, Mahoney has a lot on his plate, and his plate is never more crowded than on the day of a home game. His main role is to make sure that the media covering the game—including TV, radio, Web sites, newspapers, and more—have all that they need. That means working for days ahead of time to prepare notes, stats, and player biographies. He arranges interviews with players and coaches, while also writing numerous articles of his own for the school Web site.

On game day, that workload climbs.

"A home game is my biggest day," said Mahoney, who has been at UCSB since 1984. He has also worked in pro sports for the Oakland A's. "I have to prepare the script for the public-address announcer and make sure that the people who are in charge of the shot clock, official scoring, and scoreboard are all lined up and ready to go. I have to arrange for student **interns** to run stats and information to media who need them. And I have to prepare the postgame press conference with the coach and players."

And all that before the whistle blows on the first bucket of the game.

Mahoney has also spent time with TV producers at the arena, helping them pick locations for their cameras that will not interfere with other UCSB game operations. He has welcomed his counterparts from the other school, making sure they are treated properly. Media relations people don't get to root for their team; they have to act neutrally and professionally.

During the pregame **shootaround** as players are warming up, Mahoney usually sits with visiting TV people to fill them in on his team and its players. It might seem as if the TV guys have all those stats and info in their heads, but they get a lot of it from media relations people like Mahoney.

Mahoney will check in with local media covering the game, especially the hometown newspapers. These are the people in the media he is closest to. Some have been covering the UCSB Gauchos almost as long as Mahoney has been there. They are friends away from the arena, but on game day, the reporters are chasing stories, and Mahoney wants to make sure they get the stories he wants them to get.

Mahoney waits in the background as Coach Bob Williams is interviewed by local radio. As the media director, Mahoney tries to stay on top of whatever his coaches and players are saying to the media.

The TV people want to interview the UCSB head coach. That means going into the locker room and convincing the coach to give them a couple of minutes at this most crucial pregame time. Being polite but firm is a big part of life in media relations. Not everyone wants to cooperate but it's his job to make sure they understand how important it is. As it happens, coach Bob Williams is used to helping Mahoney do his job and the interview goes smoothly as Mahoney watches.

Mahoney keeps one eye on the action on the court, and one on the story he is writing as the game goes on.

Finally, the arena is full and the teams are on the court. At this point, after all of this pregame work is done, Mahoney says, the game is actually the quietest part. He can watch with the rest of the fans, though he is always ready to deal with anything that comes up or with requests from the TV or radio people.

When the game ends, the work frenzy starts again. As the SID, Mahoney hosts the postgame press conference, arranging for his coach and some of his players to attend, whether they won or lost. That means getting up in front of the cameras himself. A shy person will not get far in the media relations business. Following the press conference, which he helps conduct like a bandleader, he helps track down stats for reporters or answer questions from his staff.

Then he has to write a game story for the UCSB athletic department Web site, make sure that all the reporters have their needs met, check with his interns to make sure they did their jobs, and deal with any final crises. Finally, long after the school's Thunderdome arena is empty, he can head home. For Mahoney and any sports media relations professional, long days at the office are just part of the job . . . and part of the fun.

After a long day at the gym, with the last story filed and all the media requests fulfilled, Mahoney can finally call it a night.

Words To Understand

external communications: stories and news provided to people and places outside of one's own organization

videography: using video to tell stories

Getting Started

CHAPTER 1

In just about every pro and college sports organization, there is an entire department of people whose job it is to help those organizations tell their stories to the world. They are the media relations professionals. Media relations people are the behind-the-scenes connecting force between the players and teams and the media that cover them. Media relations experts work for their teams and schools, not for the media, but they have to understand both sides of that coin. The teams and schools want their story told their way; the media want to dig in and tell the story their own way. A media relations professional helps the media do their job while also knowing that protecting his organization is his number one task.

As you'll see in this book, working in media relations can be fun and involved, but it takes a lot of time and energy. You work around the spotlight, but are rarely in it. You are not the story; you are the person behind the storytellers. But for anyone who loves sports, being in media relations can be an exciting, if tiring, career. You are around sports and athletes, you are at the center of the action on game day, but you will work long hours and sometimes have to swallow your life as a "fan." The path to success in all these careers starts in school.

Studying and practicing writing of all kinds is vital to prepare for any sports communications career.

Education

Planning for a career in sports media relations can certainly start in high school. The most important classes to focus on at that point are in English language and composition. At every level of media relations, whether working in college or the pros, writing skill is vital.

All the experts agree: Nothing is more important than writing.

"Writing is the key piece," said Tami Cutler, a sports information director at Wichita

State University. "You can get experience writing in school that will pay off down the road."

UCSB's Mahoney expands on that point.

"The most important skill is the ability to write. I can teach someone to speak and introduce a press conference, but teaching to write is harder. If you don't have a solid base level of writing, it's very hard. So much of what we do is writing, from press releases to game recaps to work on the Web site, and much more. If you're on a college campus, and your grammar is poor, you'll hear about it from professors, too!"

The writing you do should not be limited to class assignments. Work on your school newspaper or Web site. Volunteer to cover high school sports for smaller, local media. Does your school have a video news report? Find out how to become the sports reporter. As we'll see, many media relations pros come to their jobs through journalism. And knowing how journalists and reporters work will be a key asset for you in media relations.

With writing as your base from high school, college offers a wealth of opportunities for further study. Look into journalism or communications courses. Take more writing classes, and also learn how to speak in front of an audience in communications classes. If you're able to add some technical skill, such as Web

Play Ball? Work Ball!

Summers between school years are a great time to find full-time internships. The upside is that they don't interfere with your classwork. The downside is that only a few sports teams need help during that time of year. Colleges are mostly shut down, while only baseball is active all summer. However, the wide range of baseball programs makes this a great possible entry. Look for a minor league near you. There are more than 240 teams in the United States and Canada.

Summer wood-bat leagues are another type of baseball program. More than 400 teams play these short-season programs. In Santa Barbara, California, the Santa Barbara Foresters have won five national championships in summer ball since 2003. Since 1995, they have used about a dozen interns each summer to help them run their games and their team and fan activities. A number of former Foresters interns have gone on to careers in many areas of pro and college sports off the field.

site design or management, or **videography** or editing, you'll make yourself more valuable.

"Plus, as we're turning to more social media, learning the basics of that will be big help," Cutler added.

Of course, learning all you can about sports is vital, too. Don't stick with just one sport. Find out all you can about all of them. The rules, the history, the key players, the top teams and schools. You will need flexibility to find your way in many different sports, so the sooner you can start building that knowledge base, the better.

When you get to college, should you major in sports management? Some experts will say that this is a good path, while

others point to majors such as communications, journalism, or business administration. With those latter choices, you can gain your sports media experience in internships or part-time jobs. If the sports management major at your college helps you find internships, however, that could be a good reason to follow that path.

These interns working for Bill Mahoney at UCSB had a front-row seat, and many in-game responsibilities.

Internships Are Key

Across the board, experts in the field say that the most important part of any future media relations education is through internships. They provide hands-on learning, but they do have to be done in your free time away from the classroom. Internships are usually not paid, but they can be enormously valuable.

"What you get is on-the-job training," said Tyler Geivett, the assistant athletic director for **external communications** at Loyola Marymount University (LMU) in Los Angeles. "You can't know what it's like until you do it; until you're under stress and a time deadline, you won't get a feel for it. An ability to step

One of Kirk Reynolds' duties is helping the Pac-12 network cover major sporting events, such as college football bowl games, here featuring Stanford of the Pac-12.

into those shoes through an internship is vital. It also gives you a chance to build a relationship with a mentor."

Kirk Reynolds knows about internships. While an undergraduate at UCSB, he worked for Mahoney. Following graduation, he got an internship with the NBA's Los Angeles Lakers. He later worked for the Oakland A's. He became the media relations director for the San Francisco 49ers, and is now a vice president of the Pac-12 Networks, the TV arm of the Pac-12 Conference.

"The key for me, particularly for a young person, is that you get a lot of people wanting to get jobs in sports," he said. "They'll send their resume in and the reason they get looked at is by establishing how different they are from the others, whether that is work experiences, internships, contacts, etc. So be sure to do things that are related to sports. Working at a department store is fine, but it's not relevant to sports. If you're hiring someone in sports, you're going to look at a kid who interned in the athletic department or at a TV station sports department or worked on a student newspaper covering sports. They have to have a level of relevant experience. That's what will open the doors. You can't do it without it. Classes in school are just not enough."

Finding Internships

Like finding a job, finding an internship takes persistence, contacts, and patience. You'll need a good resume; work with your teachers or online resources to build one. Tap into your network of friends and relatives. Does anyone know someone at a sports team or school athletic department? Or with a sports media company? A personal connection will go much farther in getting an internship than a resume sent blind.

Start with your school. Do they have contacts with local organizations? What about alumni that now work in sports, locally or elsewhere? Contact them politely and find out if they might be able to help.

Don't expect to hear "yes" the first time (or the tenth time!) you try. Getting a job in sports is very popular these days; media relations is a well-defined job with a great need for interns to do real work. Teams and schools can afford to be choosy, so they'll be looking for someone with writing experience, sports expertise, and an attitude that says, "I can work in a professional atmosphere."

Remember, though, that an internship is not your ticket to the Super Bowl. These jobs are for beginners. You'll do photocopying. You'll fetch coffee. You'll be a messenger or have to file hundreds of digital images. You won't be courtside for the Final Four or in the press box at the Super Bowl. But that's how you start in this business: at the bottom, working your way up. Everyone currently working in media relations has made coffee and stood at a photocopy machine for hours. It's the first step for everyone.

Wichita State's Tami Cutler (second from left) was part of the media staff at the 2014 NCAA Men's Final Four, when the Shockers went on a great run through the tournament.

Other Skills You'll Need

Along with writing skills and persistence, other factors are very helpful to anyone with an eye on media relations.

"You need to be a people person, able to work with a lot of different people," said Tami Cutler.

An outgoing, positive personality will work well in media relations. A shy, quiet person who does not like to speak in public will have a harder time breaking into this kind of business.

Tim Mead has been with the Los Angeles Angels for 35 years and is now the vice president of communications. He backs up the importance of what he calls interpersonal skills. "You'll be dealing with all sorts of people, different ages, different backgrounds, from different places around the world," he said. "Everything from upset fans to players with needs. You have to be a master of being a jack-of-all-trades."

Mead adds that "a work ethic is very important, too. We're not mechanized doing the same thing every day. Our day can turn on a dime. You have to be ready to be flexible and do whatever the situation calls for."

Indeed, in both pro and college sports, the demands on media professionals, especially during the sports season, are intense.

"You'll work strange hours, nights, and weekends," said

Cutler. "True, you are often at a sporting event, so it's not all bad. But when you work in sports, you have to really enjoy it because you won't get paid a lot. You have to love your job. Also, you should build your time management skills. You get pulled in many directions, so you need to be good at managing tasks."

Having a passion for the work will help with this aspect of this career. However, simply loving sports is not enough. You have to be willing to step out in front of people, ask for what you need, and get things done. You also have to understand that being in media relations, you are not the star—the team or school is.

Text-Dependent Questions

1. What is the number one skill the experts say is vital for this work?
2. Name one thing you'll need to find an internship.
3. Name one of the things mentioned as possible work for interns that is not very exciting.

Research Project

Find a university or college near you and look at their list of sports information positions. See how many there are and how their jobs are divided up. What are their titles? Do they have bios online? Read more about them and their backgrounds.

Words To Understand

buffer: a person or a thing that comes between opposing forces

compliance: the act of following rules and procedures; in this case, the act of following NCAA rules and regulations for athletes

constituencies: a specific group of people related by their connection to an organization or demographic group

inconsolable: unable to be consoled; extremely sad

Hard at Work

CHAPTER 2

Bill Mahoney's experience on game day (see "Introduction") is only one aspect of life in media relations. Every media relations pro has dozens of those days every sports season, running around doing five things at once while juggling staff, reporters, athletes, and more. That's true whether the person is working in college sports or in the pro ranks. Here's more information about the day-to-day lives of people working in sports media relations.

Back to Campus

Colleges of all sizes have athletic departments. The top universities in Division I often have large staff, with several people working on the bigger sports like football or men's basketball. Finding a job in one of those often means working your way up from within that school, or working at smaller schools and moving up.

In fact, smaller schools might offer more opportunities for people starting in their careers. The workload is still intense, but the audiences are smaller. The staff is often smaller, too, so you get a chance to try out just about every kind of media relations task.

"At a smaller school, you might wear lots of different kinds of hats," said LMU's Tyler Geivett. "At a larger school, you might specialize. For example, I do public address announcements at our baseball games, I create the game day press releases, and I even cut [edit] video. You don't need to be the best at those tasks, but you have to have the ability to adapt and want to learn."

College media relations departments juggle many different sports. The NCAA has programs for 23 different sports. College SIDs like Mahoney or staffers like Geivett move through the year, changing sports as the seasons change.

Working in college sports has another layer to consider. The NCAA places a large set of rules on both athletes and staff people alike. Knowing those rules is a big part of the job of anyone working in any part of a collegiate athletic department. That can sometimes stifle creativity.

"In college, there is a lot more restriction on what you can do than in the pros," said Reynolds, who has worked for

One of the many hats Tyler Geivett wears at LMU is being the announcer for the school's baseball team.

many years in both parts of the sports world. "The NCAA has to follow guidelines that from a PR [public relations] standpoint limit some of the things we can do. On the conference side and on the network side, there are so many things that you'd think would be a good deal, but you have to run through **compliance**. And sometimes they say you can't follow through with your idea because it would go against NCAA rules."

Becoming part of a college media relations department will mean learning all of the many rules that have to do with athletes, teams, sponsors, boosters, and academics. Part of your job will be making sure those rules are followed.

My Players, My Friends?

One issue that young media relations people face is the question of how close to get to the student-athletes. Interns and those starting their working lives are often the same age or just a bit older than the students. The temptation to become friends is one that most experts say should be avoided. Being friendly is good, of course, and being positive and helpful is as well. But crossing the line and going out with student-athletes or spending a lot of time with them outside the athletic circle can lead to conflicts.

"When I first started in this business, I was just 22 and I went out with students and got to be friends," remembered Mahoney. "And it took me time to learn that that was not the right way to go. I teach our interns and employees to keep the barriers up so that they can do the job. For example, we had an intern at our 2004 national championship soccer game, a game that we lost, who was so **inconsolable** after the loss that he could not do the job. I had to step in, actually. That's not what we expect of our people. They have to be professional no matter what the results."

However, being around young people is still a plus for many who work in college athletics.

"Getting to know the student athletes is one of my favorite parts," said Wichita State's Tami Cutler. "They keep me young. And they help me keep up with the latest music, too!"

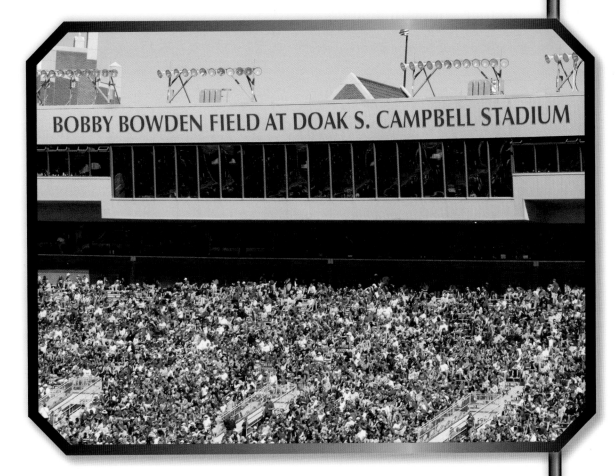

The media's home at the stadium is usually a large press box located high above the playing field.

Cutler points out another great benefit of working in college sports: Once you are part of a sport's media team, you often travel with that team to away games.

"I get paid to go to baseball games and go to other cool places and travel, even to Hawaii, all while I work and get paid," Cutler said with a laugh.

For Tami Cutler, traveling from chilly Kansas to sunny Hawaii is a big bonus of her job.

In the Pros

Media relations in college retains some of the feel of the college experience. The players are not paid, they know they will soon move on, and they are there, in many cases, much more for the love of the game than for any financial reward.

In pro sports, the game changes.

Media relations workers in the pro ranks face many of the same challenges as in the college ranks, but with much more pressure, given the amount of money that is at stake. The distance between the workers and the highly paid players can seem greater, too.

One of the hardest things for people new to the pros is to avoid the sense of awe from being around people who are, frankly, known around the world. You might be in the locker room or on the team plane with world superstars, but you cannot be a starstruck fan. You have to act professionally at all times.

"I don't want to turn off someone's excitement," said the Angels' Tim Mead. "I've been here 35 years and I'm still a fan. But you have to learn to turn that off when you come in the door. Also, once you're around the big stars, you learn they are people just like you, no matter how big their bank account is. You develop a business relationship."

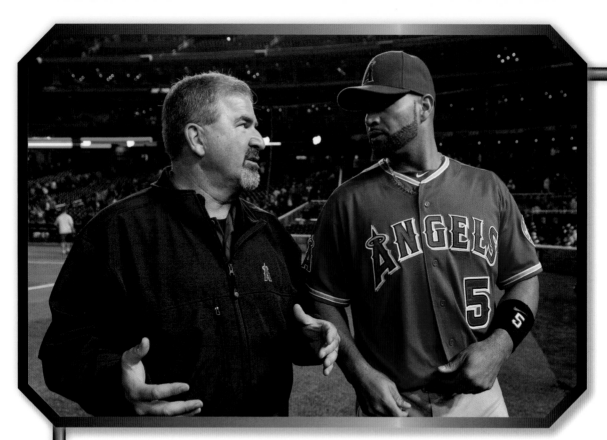

Tim Mead makes sure that superstars like Albert Pujols can focus on their jobs on the field.

In the pros, media relations people act as a **buffer** between the stars and the media. Most interviews are done with a media person present, or even listening in on telephone interviews. The pros come with the added layer of agents, people who represent the players, and who often want a story told a certain way. Media relations people in the pros must remember they work for the team, not the player or the agent.

In both pro and college, media relations people must also deal with fans. In the pros, the work is magnified, and every word put out by the team must be carefully chosen to make sure that the team's reputation is protected. When dealing with fans—excited or irate—media people have to remember to be positive and helpful, a task that is sometimes difficult.

"It can be a challenge, but the first move is to be a good listener," said Mead. "Everybody wants an outlet, they want someone to blame. So be a good listener and try to pick up on what their anger or frustrations are, so you can address them. Let the fire burn out a little bit. You have to protect the club first, but try to be understanding. Then you can try to give a counter explanation."

However, even with the challenges of long hours or upset fans, do media relations people share in the joy of victory when their team brings home a longed-for championship? After their work is done, yes, they do. After all, media relations people began their work because they love sports...and they love to win.

Be the Connector

In college or the pros, media relations people are the bridge between inside the team and outside the team. "You need to be able to connect with many different **constituencies**," says the Pac-12's Kirk Reynolds. "You have to be the connector. In fact, I'm seeing a shift in expectations from athletic directors to be more proactive in the PR efforts in college. You need to be creative and find those opportunities instead of just waiting for them to come to you."

That means paying attention to what the media is writing about and "pitching" stories that will help your team or its players. Top college football programs, for example, often put

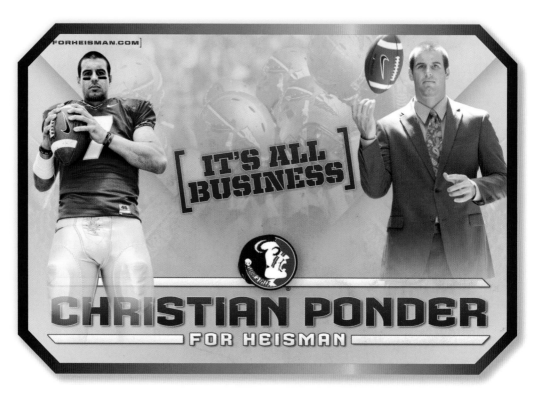

College athletic departments become salespeople for their athletes, putting on campaigns for big awards, such as this (unsuccessful) 2010 campaign from Florida State for Christian Ponder.

on big PR campaigns to help a star player gain votes for the Heisman Trophy, given to the top college football player. Or they will make sure that media know about a community service project that a team is organizing, which helps put that team in a positive light.

In pro sports, the connection might need a little diplomacy. "There might be a writer that wants to do a story with a player, but that player doesn't want to do it," says Reynolds, who worked in the NFL for the 49ers. "But you as a PR person think that it is a good idea, so you've got to have the skills to convince that player that this is a good thing and we need him to do it. You're in the middle of all of it, making connections."

Text-Dependent Questions

1. What is the name of the organization that sets rules for college sports?

2. What does Reynolds say a good media relations person should be?

3. What did Mahoney say about relations between college media people and student-athletes?

Research Project

Think up a half-dozen story ideas about your favorite team that you'd like to see written. Then write up a short proposal email that you might send to a reporter covering the team.

Words To Understand

learning curve: a measurement of the process of learning a new skill or area of expertise; usually used with "steep" to show that someone learned a lot in a short time

Realities of the Workplace

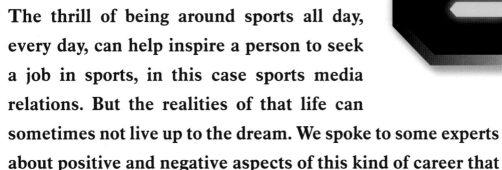

The thrill of being around sports all day, every day, can help inspire a person to seek a job in sports, in this case sports media relations. But the realities of that life can sometimes not live up to the dream. We spoke to some experts about positive and negative aspects of this kind of career that should be considered as you look toward the future.

Never Know What You Might Get

If you are just a fan of baseball or basketball, that might not be enough. You have to be ready, especially when working in college sports, to take on challenges in areas where you might not be comfortable.

"I started working at UCSB and had never seen water polo,"

Learn the sports: You might be part of the record-keeping or stats crew at any event.

said LMU's Tyler Geivett. "I'd never seen a game outside of the Olympics. But I took on the sports information work for the sport and went through a steep **learning curve**. So you should know the main sports, but don't be afraid to take on something you don't know much about. Be honest with who you're working for, and say I don't know but I'm willing to tackle it."

Similarly, when you are in a pro sports situation, you might have your eye on handling player interviews, but be asked to do stats instead. Be ready and flexible and that can work out for you. Being afraid to try new things can be a roadblock.

"Get in the door," said Tim Mead of the Angels. "Get in the door and see what happens."

Women in Media Relations

Sports for women, especially at the college level, have skyrocketed in popularity, influence, and importance in recent decades. It's still not on the level of men's sports,

Women can definitely find a place in media relations. Here's a UCSB intern shooting video of the basketball team in action.

however, and finding a role in what is often a male-dominated world can be challenging. However, all the experts said that gender should not be a barrier for a hard-working, professional person who wants to be in media relations.

Tami Cutler of Wichita State has been a top person in the field for 15 years and she has seen improvements all around.

"When I started 15 years ago, I was given baseball to handle, but there were four girls that year in our office, so one of us was going to need to handle it. But in the past, if there was one guy in an office of women, he would have gotten baseball. In college and the low minors especially, you're traveling on the road, often on long bus rides with lots of college kids. That's maybe not what all those guys want, a girl on the bus. But I was thrilled when I got baseball because it's such a big deal here at Wichita State.

"Now I think it's not as hard for women. I see many more women working with baseball than I did before. I think at the pro level it's harder. But in college, we see a lot more women in media relations. And that's not true in other areas of sports."

Finding the right mentors can help both men and women, but for women, those internships and having a chance to prove their skills can be especially important. Building your writing and communications skills, of course, are the first step.

Tami Cutler watches over one of her volleyball players; helping players learn to give interviews is part of the job of the college media relations professional.

Money and Time

Pro athletes are, for the most part, millionaires or will be soon. College athletes are usually on full scholarship and the best of them are well taken care of and have dreams of joining the pro ranks.

That is not true of people working in media relations.

"This is not a great job if you want to get wealthy," says UCSB's Bill Mahoney. "You're going to hit a ceiling. It's a great job if you like sports and you like to write. And you can make a nice living after you put in a few years and move up. But the money is just not going to make you rich."

And to make that money, you will often have to work long or difficult hours. "The

Mahoney of UCSB has been able to combine his communications skills with his love of sports to craft a long and successful career.

hours are hard," said Kirk Reynolds of the Pac-12. "In the pros or college, you're working a ton, basically every day during the season. There are not a lot of days off so you have to prepare for that. You're basically always on call, especially in the pros. If something goes wrong, you have to be ready to deal with

Another day at the ballpark also means more time away from family, a challenge faced by media pros.

things right away. The work-life balance is a challenge."

Do you want a job with steady hours and the chance for a meaningful advance in pay? Or are you ready to put aside your family time and perhaps dreams of a big payday? Anyone considering a career in media relations has to ask those questions and be ready with answers.

However, on the positive side, Mead, Reynolds, and other experts interviewed for this book noted that communications skills are often easily transferred to other industries. Learning to take on the role of spokesperson, in-house writer, and professional storyteller can lead to opportunities in almost any other business. Keeping your options open is always a good idea, no matter how much you love sports today.

Understanding the Other Side

In sports media relations, along with the athletes, your day-to-day associates will be members of the professional media (and/or college media for people working at universities). They are the other people you serve, along with your team or university. They can be demanding, asking questions you don't or can't answer. They can make requests that can be hard to fulfill. They can sometimes make your life and your job difficult. But you have to work with them, so learning how they do their jobs and what their expectations are is important.

Learn the deadlines for local papers or local sports news broadcasts. If you provide your information within their deadlines, they will respond positively. Understand that they are

Reporters need time with the athletes to do their jobs. The team media professionals understand that, but keep their focus on their main responsibility—to their players and owners.

trying to tell their readers or viewers a story through their own viewpoint, not yours. You have to maintain the point of view of the organization, so you should not get too worked up if the journalists don't agree.

Also, there will be words and terms that you'll need to learn to be able to converse with them, everything from "two-shot" (a video image of an interview, for example), to B-roll (video footage taken outside of game action to use as background), to columns vs. features vs. profiles in newspaper writing.

Sponsor Relations

Some of the most important people to any sports organization don't play a game or buy a ticket. But many sports and colleges could not survive without them. Sponsors bring the money that makes sports go. Pro teams and college athletic departments have separate staff in sports marketing who see to the happiness and care of these sponsors, but media relations people need to be very well versed in their organization's sponsors, too. If Pepsi sponsors your team, as they do in the NFL, you shouldn't show up in the press box drinking a Coca-Cola. If your team wears Nike, don't come to a practice in Pony-brand shoes. But that's just the personal; there is also the media relations work of making sure that brand and sponsor logos are properly displayed or included in appropriate places in team media materials. Knowing who is on your team's roster is vital, but knowing who is on your team's roster of sponsors is also key.

Also, you need to develop the right kind of relationships with journalists. Though you might become friendly, you have to be professional at all times.

"The media we have here have been here for a while," said Mahoney. "So we've built up a lot of trust. I never mislead them. If there is something I can't tell them, I tell them that. Trust is the key word on both sides of that. Both sides have to understand each other's jobs."

Bottom line: The more you can understand what print, radio, and television journalists are and do, the better you can do your job in media relations.

Text-Dependent Questions

1. Did Geivett say you should stick with one sport or be flexible?

2. True or false: You will almost always become rich working in media relations.

3. What does Cutler think of the future for women in sports media relations?

Research Project

Find a local journalist—Web, newspaper, TV, radio—and see if they'll do a short interview with you. Ask them about how they do their jobs. Ask about how they relate to public relations and media relations professionals. What are the relationships like? How have they changed?

Words To Understand

boilerplate: a standard set of text and information that an organization puts at the end of every press release

objective: material written based solely on the facts of a situation

subjective: material written from a particular point of view, choosing facts to suit the opinion

The Nitty-Gritty

CHAPTER 4

Every pro team and every college athletics program will have a different story to tell. No matter what logo you're working for, many of the skills and projects you'll undertake in media relations are similar from place to place. One reason is that journalists expect a certain set of information in predictable ways. Another is to standardize what each team or college produces so their league or conference knows that it's getting the same information from each team or school.

Here's a look at some of the basic products you'll create while working in media relations. See if you can find examples from your favorite team or school; their Web sites will have most if not all of these forms of communication.

The Press Release

This is one of the oldest and most accepted forms of providing information to the media. Press releases are just what their name says—a release of information to the press. Media of all sizes depend on these releases to get basic information on which to base their stories or their future reporting. By providing the same information at one time to all media parties, the press release also saves media relations people a lot of time, essentially answering all the key questions the media have at the same time.

A press release can be issued for just about any reason. In college sports, a release might announce the hiring of a new coach, the signing of a new recruit, or even big news from the pros about school alumni. Pro sports teams put out numerous releases as well, including injury reports, hirings and firings, announcements of player fines or penalties, or stories about a team's good works in the community.

A standard press release is not very long, usually 1-3 pages, double-spaced. It includes all the basic key points right at the beginning, much like a thesis statement in an essay or the "lead" in a general news story. The tone of just about every press release is positive and upbeat. The press release writer is trying to encourage the media to report this story to their readers or viewers, so they try to cast it in the best possible light. The release does not lie, but it does present the truth in the best way for the organization. It is not journalism, but information provided by an interested party. It is written in such a way, however, that should a media outlet choose, they could run it word for word. Many small media outlets, such as smaller newspapers, run many press releases this way.

Because the release might appear as delivered, it is very important the media relations department produce a well-written piece. Remember what the experts said about the importance of writing? Here is where it starts.

Press releases also generally provide some background about the organization at the end of the release (text known as "**boilerplate**") as well as contact information, should the media have follow-up questions. Media relations people quickly learn that crafting a press release is one of the tasks they'll take on most often.

The Game Story

At just about every sports event, reporters from various outlets attend in person to watch the game and interview athletes. They create a news story of that game (who won, who lost, what happened), along with feature stories surrounding the event (records broken, interesting people, etc.). They depend on media relations people to help them with stats, background, and introductions. But nearly all organizations also produce their own game story, used on the team or school Web site or other outlets. A person is assigned to write that story for every game or event. The deadline is usually very soon after the event. So writing well is important…so is writing quickly. (Author's note: I once needed to craft an 800-word story on the MVP of Super Bowl XXXI that was due 20 minutes after the game ended…and that included time interviewing Brett Favre, the award winner.)

A game story produced by a media relations department will try to "spin" the story to benefit its team or school.

"When a team is winning, writing game stories is fun and easy," said LMU's Tyler Geivett. "But when your team loses, you have to work to find the positive angles of the story and highlight those."

The "official" game story does not hide a loss, but it probably does tell the story differently than an **objective** journalist might. Media relations writing is **subjective**, telling facts but with a particular point of view.

Game stories do call for the same skills as a journalist, though. You need to understand the sport, watch the action for key turning points, and tell the readers what happened, in crisp, easy-to-follow sentences. You might also interview athletes from both teams to get their reactions for your readers. Writing well, writing fast, and writing with a positive spin: The writing skills needed by media relations people pile up!

The Interview

Media relations people often have to interview athletes following the game and provide key quotes from those interviews to the media. So learning how to interview is an important skill. The best way is to simply practice; the more interviews you do, the better and smoother you'll become. Try to craft direct questions but not ones that can be an-swered "yes" or "no." Listen carefully to the answers; don't just go down your list regardless of what they say. A great

Make a plan before you start any interview, but be ready to scrap the plan, too.

Working with Social Media

The rise of social media has radically changed some aspects of the media relations person's job. You are always on, 24-7, and might have to respond quickly to lightning-fast news.

Tyler Geivett of LMU offered some thoughts on how young media relations people should approach this issue:

We have all the social media platforms here at LMU. It's certainly something that I think young people should focus on, but it changes a lot. They also should have an understanding of the positives and the negatives. We talk to our student-athletes all the time, to make sure they understand that once it's out, it's out forever. But it also creates opportunities that we didn't have before. The negative side is that it's made our job a bit more difficult. We have to watch the athletes to make sure they're not breaking any rules. There's more to monitor, but there's an upside and a downside to it."

interview is a guided conversation, not a list of Q's and A's.

In the heat of a postgame interview, remember the player's mood. If they won, interviews are much easier. But if they lost, it will be harder for you to coax good information or stories out of them. Prompt them with incidents from the game that might highlight a key moment. Refer to times and plays ("In the third inning, you faced John Smith with two on and no out…") so the player can comment on specifics. People reading about the games want to hear something they didn't see themselves or hear on TV or radio already, so if you can take the reader into the players' heads, you'll probably have a good interview.

However, unlike media members, the media relations staff will always try to find the positive in any situation. It's not your job to publicize trouble or bad feelings; it's your job to put the best possible light on any situation.

It's a fine line, of course, but one that you'll find easier the more you walk it.

Media Guide

Every pro sports team and most major college sports departments produce an annual publication known as the media guide. This is one-stop-shopping for reporters who will cover the team regularly. The guide is added to each year, so that some pro team guides now span hundreds and hundreds of pages. Most teams still print the guides, but all provide them online as well so that now even fans can enjoy them.

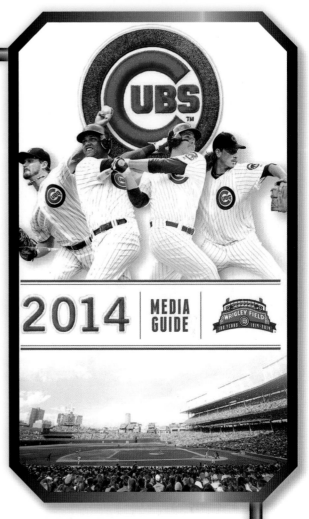

Digital or print media guides provide tons of stats for writers.

The guides include short biographies of all the players and coaches on that year's team; records and statistics of current and former teams; history stories about the team and/or school; awards the team or its players have won; and much more.

The media relations department is responsible for updating the guide each year and preparing it for publication. Understanding how books and magazines are printed is another valuable skill for up-and-coming workers in this field.

No Cheering in the Press Box

Along with knowing the physical work product you'll create—press releases, game stories, media guides, etc.—understanding the culture of the world you're entering is also important. One of the most important rules is "no cheering in the press box." No matter how excited or depressed you are about your team—pro or college—you must remain outwardly neutral.

"You just have to know the difference between wanting your team to win and staying professional," said LMU's Geivett. "I developed that while working at the Oakland A's. Separating work from being a fan, I learned that in the pros. When you work there, you're neutral, and I still tell that to our student workers. You want to see your team win, but the key for us in media relations is to find the positive."

Crisis Management

While most of the work of media relations people falls under the radar of most fans, there are times when they are called upon to be part of the story. When something goes wrong—when a player gets in trouble with the law or when a coach breaks a rule and gets fined—media relations people have to manage the crisis. They learn to tell the truth, but only as far as it does not overly harm the organization. Good media relations crisis management tries to find the positive and show the solutions, instead of re-hashing whatever caused the crisis.

"We're like the first responders when something happens," said UCSB's Mahoney. "We once had a fan run onto the basketball court during a nationally televised game. That made the national news. Another year, we had a player shove a referee during a soccer game. When something like that happens, we're the ones that take the calls from the media. That's not just here in town, we're hearing from ESPN and NBC and CNN and more."

Every media relations department will have a strategy and a plan for such crisis management. It is a delicate balance and organizations that get it right can benefit greatly. Groups that get that balance wrong can make a little problem into a big one. Working with experienced pros in this area—while watching the news to see how other places handle crisis situations—is the best way to learn this important skill.

The Future

What does the future hold for media relations? All indications are that it will continue to be a part of every college and pro sports organization. The jobs are hard to get, but they will be there.

Kirk Reynolds, the veteran media relations expert now with Pac-12 Networks, summed up the feelings of most experts.

"There's always going to be a demand for sports. We see that with the growth of the regional sports networks, and the depth of coverage of all teams. Sports is the one thing that is DVR-proof. People want to watch live events. That's created a demand for more content in all media. So there will always be positions in sports to help make those happen. As new technologies come into play, it creates new and different roles for people to play. Today's young people in these jobs have to be creative and know how to create their own content and programming. That will be a big part of any media relations job in the future."

Tim Mead of the Angels notes the change in the name of his department as a sign of the evolution of the job. "We used to be public relations, then we were media relations, and now we're communications," he said. "Communications in the future will have a wider range of responsibilities than just press releases and game stories."

If you love sports, love telling stories about sports, and have writing skills, great "people" skills, and a lot of determination, sports media relations might be the career for you.

Text-Dependent Questions

1. Name two products that media relations people usually have to produce.

2. What is the famous saying related to how media relations people should act?

3. Describe briefly what the goal of a press release is?

Research Project

Find something in the sports world in recent months that has been bad news for one team or player. Read the coverage of the event and see if you can find when a "team spokesman" or media relations expert spoke for the team. Compare what they said to what the objective journalists said. Do you see their different points of view?

Find Out More

Books

Hopwood, Maria, James Skinner, Paul Kitchin. *Sports Public Relations and Communications*. London: Taylor and Francis, 2013.

Pedersen, Paul (editor). *Routledge Handbook of Sport Communication* (Routledge International Handbooks). New York: Routledge, 2013.

Schultz, Brad, Philip H. Caskey, Craig Esherick. *Media Relations in Sports*. Morgantown, W.V.: FiT Publishing, 2013.

Web Sites

Newhouse Sports Media Center at Syracuse University
www.newhousesports.syr.edu/

Association for Women in Sports Media
www.awsmonline.org/about/Explore Health Careers

College Sports Information Directors of America
www.cosida.com/

Series Glossary of Key Terms

academic: relating to classes and studies

alumni: people who graduate from a particular college

boilerplate: a standard set of text and information that an organization puts at the end of every press release

compliance: the action of following rules

conferences: groups of schools in which schools within a group play each other frequently in sports

constituencies: a specific group of people related by their connection to an organization or demographic group

credential: a document that gives the holder permission to take part in an event in a way not open to the public

eligibility: a student's ability to compete in sports, based on grades or other school or NCAA requirements

entrepreneurs: people who start their own companies

freelance: a person who does not work full-time for a company, but is paid for each piece of work

gamer: in sports journalism, a write-up of a game

intercollegiate: something that takes places between two schools, such as a sporting event

internships: positions that rarely offer pay but provide on-the-job experience

orthopedics: the branch of medicine that specializes in preventing and correcting problems with bones and muscles

objective: material written based solely on the facts of a situation

recruiting: the process of finding the best athletes to play for a team

revenue: money earned from a business or event

spreadsheets: computer programs that calculate numbers and organize information in rows and columns

subjective: material written from a particular point of view, choosing facts to suit the opinion

Index

Credits

Courtesy Tami Cutler/Wichita State University: 23, 43; CP7Heisman.com: 36; Dollar Photo: James Steidl 40; Dreamstime.com: VGStudio 16; Diver721 31; Eric Border Van Dyke 32; Drimi 55. Mike Eliason: 8, 11, 12, 13, 19, 41, 44, 50. Courtesy Tyler Geivett/LMU Athletics: 29; Courtesy Tim Mead/Los Angeles Angels: 34; Newscom: Bill Streicher/Icon SMI 14; Christopher Trim 20; Kevin Dietsch/UPI 47; Shutterstock: Aspen Photo 26, Mike Broglio 39.

About the Author

James Buckley Jr. has worked in various parts of sports media for more than 25 years. He was an editor at *Sports Illustrated* and NFL Publishing, was the editor of *NFL Magazine*, and has written more than 100 books on sports for adults and young readers. He also volunteers as the media relations director for the Santa Barbara Foresters, a five-time national champion summer collegiate baseball team. *Thanks to Bill Mahoney at UCSB for his invaluable help.*